T0319314

Finding Freedom from Anxiety and Stress

Renew & Restore Bible Studies

Finding Freedom from Anxiety and Stress

Managing Your Emotions

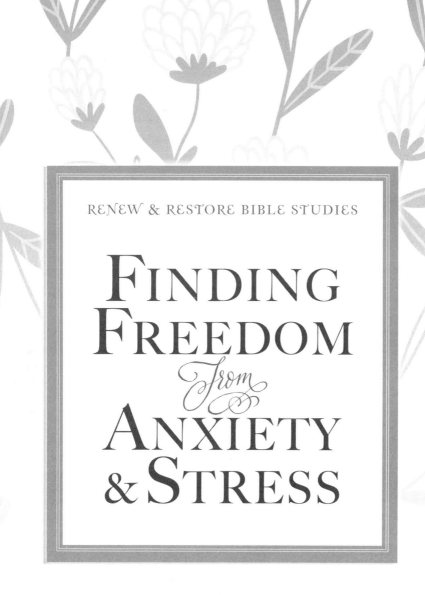

RENEW & RESTORE BIBLE STUDIES

FINDING FREEDOM *from* ANXIETY & STRESS

BY

CHRISTA KINDE

THOMAS NELSON
Since 1798

Finding Freedom from Anxiety and Stress

© 2003 Thomas Nelson

Derived from material previously published in *Living Above Worry and Stress.*

All rights reserved. No portion of this book may be reproduced, stored in a retrieval system, or transmitted in any form or by any means—electronic, mechanical, photocopy, recording, scanning, or other—except for brief quotations in critical reviews or articles, without the prior written permission of the publisher.

Published in Nashville, Tennessee, by Thomas Nelson. Thomas Nelson is a registered trademark of HarperCollins Christian Publishing, Inc.

The publishers are grateful to Christa Kinde for her collaboration, writing skills, and editorial help in developing the content for this book.

Thomas Nelson titles may be purchased in bulk for educational, business, fundraising, or sales promotional use. For information, please e-mail SpecialMarkets@ ThomasNelson.com.

Scripture quotations marked NKJV are taken from the New King James Version®. Copyright © 1982 by Thomas Nelson. Used by permission. All rights reserved.

Scripture quotations marked NCV are taken from the New Century Version®. Copyright © 2005 by Thomas Nelson. Used by permission. All rights reserved.

Scripture quotations marked NLT are taken from the Holy Bible, New Living Translation. © 1996, 2004, 2015 by Tyndale House Foundation. Used by permission of Tyndale House Publishers, Inc., Carol Stream, Illinois 60188. All rights reserved.

Any internet addresses, phone numbers, or company or product information printed in this book are offered as a resource and are not intended in any way to be or to imply an endorsement by Thomas Nelson, nor does Thomas Nelson vouch for the existence, content, or services of these sites, phone numbers, companies, or products beyond the life of this book.

ISBN 978-0-7852-4027-3 (eBook)
ISBN 978-0-7852-4022-8 (hardcover)

Cover design: Michelle Lenger
Cover illustrations: iStockphoto®
Interior design: Kristy Edwards

Printed in China

21 22 23 24 25 26 27 28 29 30   DSC   10 9 8 7 6 5 4 3 2 1

CONTENTS

INTRODUCTION

"Consider the lilies, how they grow: they neither toil nor spin; and yet I say to you, even Solomon in all his glory was not arrayed like one of these. If then God so clothes the grass, which today is in the field and tomorrow is thrown into the oven, how much more will He clothe you, O you of little faith?"

Luke 12:27–28 NKJV

The words echo back to us from years gone by. We first heard them in Vacation Bible School or from a dear Sunday school teacher—the voice of Jesus calling us to consider the lilies. The lesson is a simple one: don't worry. If God gives the flowers such pretty petals, dressing them more grandly than wealthy King Solomon could manage, He will provide for our needs, too.

Unfortunately, the call to consider the lilies is too often forgotten, left on a dusty shelf somewhere. Probably right next to the old plea to stop and smell the roses. We're too busy to stop. We're too rushed to consider. Our to-do lists are long. Our calendars are booked. Our time is money. We can't keep up.

We are busy people. We have responsibilities at work. We have responsibilities at home, at church, at school. We have responsibilities within our communities. We care for the needs of our parents, spouses, children, siblings, employers, friends. And it isn't enough to simply see to these things. We strive for perfection, yearning to "have it all." Most days, it is more than we can handle. Our hearts are overwhelmed. We are stressed out. We are worried. We dread tomorrow.

In the midst of all this everyday turmoil, our hearts long for a place of peace. We know God has promised us rest. We know He says we don't have to worry about tomorrow. He promised to calm our fears. Yet we barely have time to whisper a prayer, let alone study our Bibles. If you have been struggling, come. Let's carve out some time to explore the Scriptures and find some practical guidelines for laying aside our worries and fears, our stress and anxiety. You really can discover a place of peace.

THE PURPOSE OF THIS SERIES

The *Renew & Restore Bible Studies* are designed to help you connect with God through His Word, give Him your burdens and troubles, and experience the healing power of His promises. Whether you are studying individually or with a group, this book will give you the chance to reflect on key Scripture passages and consider how they apply to your life and circumstances. So pull out your Bible and a pen, and get ready to enter into quiet time with God.

FOR LEADERS

If you are leading a group through this study guide or engaging in individual study, please see the Leader's Guide at the back of the book for suggested answers and insights to the reflection questions.

START AT HOME

A prayer of one overwhelmed with trouble,
pouring out problems before the LORD.
LORD, hear my prayer!
Listen to my plea!
Don't turn away from me
in my time of distress.
Bend down to listen,
and answer me quickly when I call to you.
For my days disappear like smoke.
PSALM 102:1–3 NLT

Sometimes we don't realize how busy we really are. Because we're right in the middle of living our lives, it feels quite normal. Sure, if we stop to think about it, we could stand to slow down our hectic pace a little, but there's just a lot going on right now. As it is, we don't get everything done in a day that we want to, so it doesn't make sense to slow down even

1

more. Besides, we can handle it, right?

Oftentimes for me, I don't realize how busy my life has gotten until I visit my parents' home. They still live in the old brick farmhouse where I grew up. It's situated on ten acres, near a quaint little Scandinavian town. Whenever I go back for a visit, I'm amazed at how quietly they live.

They have to drive to the next town to do any real shopping. The closest fast-food restaurant is twenty minutes away. So is the nearest freeway. Usually, though, they just stay home. Dad keeps a vegetable garden, and Mom has a rose garden. They eat their own fruit and vegetables in season and can the leftovers. They sit and watch the birds that visit their feeders. The pace of their life is steady. Their home is a quiet haven from a busy world.

We know from the Bible that "God is not the author of confusion but of peace" (1 Corinthians 14:33 NKJV). Although we don't all desire to live out in the country, we each want our home to be a place of peace, a respite from the daily confusion that surrounds us. So how can we cultivate this restful space in the midst of our hectic lives?

1. *In the space below, or in the page at the end of the session if you need more room, list out the responsibilities that you regularly see to. How many hours do you work? What are your responsibilities around the home? What activities do you attend on a regular basis? How are you involved in your community? Who depends on you?*

2. Look at the list of the people you are responsible for and the jobs you must do. Do you feel overwhelmed by all these responsibilities? Do any of them (or all of them put together) make you feel stressed or anxious?

3. In the midst of all this business and busyness, what would you say are the most important things in your life? Can all of them be found on your list?

4. *Fear, anxiety, and stress are not a part of God's plan for our lives. What is His plan for us? Read Jeremiah 29:11–14. What promises do these verses make?*

5. *Look at David's prayer in Psalm 102:1–3 at the beginning of this session. How is he feeling? What parts of this passage resonate with you?*

6. *When God made you, what did He have in mind for His workmanship? Look in Ephesians 2:10. What do you think these good works could be, and how might you fulfill them in your own life?*

Digging Deeper

When our responsibilities and stresses threaten to overwhelm us, God can offer us shelter from the storm. He wants to be our safe haven in the midst of the chaos. Let's examine a few Scriptures that explore both our connection with God and the true meaning of home. If you are in a group or own multiple Bible translations, look at how different translations add new meaning to the text. Which passages stand out to you, and in what ways could you implement the messages in your daily life?

- Psalm 91:1–2
- Proverbs 3:33
- Isaiah 28:16
- Isaiah 32:18
- Matthew 7:25
- John 14:1–2

PONDER & PRAY

Are you feeling busy? Is the busyness too much to handle? As you pray this week, follow David's example and cry out to the Lord. Pour out your heart before Him and tell Him about the strain you are under. Ask God to help you see what is important to *Him* in your days. Then ask God to guide you in organizing your time. His leading and inspiration will turn you to the path He has prepared for you.

ADDITIONAL NOTES &
PRAYER REQUESTS

SESSION 2

FEAR AND TREMBLING

Whenever I am afraid,
I will trust in You.
PSALM 56:3 NKJV

When I was a child, I was afraid of the dark. I couldn't go to bed without my teddy bear, ingeniously named Teddy, and my night-light. I would snuggle Teddy close and look at the nightlight's orange glow, and they would comfort me even in the midst of the dark, scary night.

Of course, we don't leave our fears behind in childhood; we simply exchange them for grown-up fears. Are you afraid of rejection? Of saying the wrong thing at the wrong time? Of losing your job? Are you afraid your kids will start doing drugs or get in with the wrong crowd? Are you afraid the diagnosis will be cancer? That your parents, friends, colleagues will never become Christians? Are you afraid of divorce? Are you afraid of the outside threats that can loom large—thieves, kidnappers, murderers, rapists, and terrorists? Are you afraid of loneliness? Growing old? Not having enough time? Are you afraid of what people think about you? Are you afraid God doesn't really love you anymore? Are you still afraid of the dark?

Did you know the children of Israel had nightlights? The entire nation was afraid of the dark. In ancient times, the oil lamps that lit homes were kept burning all night long. It was so important to keep that lamp burning that poor people would spend their money on oil first, even if there wasn't enough left to buy food! God knew His people needed certain reassurances. So when they were uprooted from their homes and forced to pitch their tents in barren landscapes each night, they were comforted by the presence of a pillar of fire. The glow it cast over the sleeping camp reminded the children of Israel their Constant Companion was near.

1. *Were you ever afraid of the dark? Did you have nightmares when you were little? Do you still have them now? What comfort do Psalm 91:5 and Proverbs 3:24 provide?*

2. *These days, just watching the evening news can leave us a bit uneasy. Planes crash, diseases spread, wars rage, climates change, and disasters hit. When all the news seems to be bad news, how can we stay strong and steadfast? Look at Psalm 112:7.*

3. *God thinks of everything, and His promises can comfort our hearts. Gossip and rumors are vicious, and misunderstandings can injure a relationship. Some of us are afraid of what people might say or think about us, but what does Isaiah 51:7 promise?*

4. *Some of us are afraid of pain and death. With so much violence and destruction in the world today, it feels like anything can strike at any time. What does Jesus tell His believers in Luke 12:4? Do you find His words reassuring? Why or why not?*

We tend to think of the men and women we find in the Bible as brave. Their reputations are filled with honor, courage, and faithfulness. However, if we take a quick look through the Scriptures, it isn't hard to discover people's fears.

Eve was afraid she was missing out on something (Genesis 3:2–5). Moses was afraid to speak in public (Exodus 4:10). David was afraid his sin would be discovered (2 Samuel 11). Esther was afraid of admitting her family background (Esther 2:10). The disciples were afraid of asking dumb questions (Mark 9:32). Jairus was afraid his child would die (Luke 8:41–42). Martha was afraid of disappointing her guests (Luke 10:40). Paul was afraid people wouldn't believe him (Acts 9:26).

God often calls us to take courage, even in the face of fear and opposition, and do what we know we should. The ultimate honor is given to the man or woman who fears God above all else.

5. In the face of everything from small qualms to our worst fears,
    Jesus has one thing to say to us. Turn to Mark 5:36. What does our
    Lord urge us to do?

6. Matthew 10:29–31 offers a very good reminder of why we don't
    need to be afraid. What is it?

7. *Still, the fact remains that sometimes we just can't help but be afraid. What do we need to remind ourselves whenever our fears creep in? Let's consider Isaiah 12:2. What declarations and promises in the verse can we lean on?*

8. *No matter what might happen on this earth, what does God have in store for you in the end? Write down your own answer to the question, then consult Luke 12:32.*

Digging Deeper

So many passages in the Bible are an encouragement to those whose hearts tremble. Let's explore some of the passages that encourage us to leave our fears behind. If you can, look at how different Bible translations address these Scriptures. Are there any verses that you find particularly comforting?

- Genesis 15:1
- Deuteronomy 31:8
- Psalm 27:1
- Isaiah 41:10
- John 14:27

Ponder & Pray

When we find ourselves hindered by our fears, we are in good company. Many of the men and women in the Bible had to be calmed by the words "Fear not." Lay out your secret dread before your loving Lord. He already knows what you hide in your heart, and He longs to take away your fears. Pray that God will give you the grace to trust Him, no matter what turns your life may take.

ADDITIONAL NOTES &
PRAYER REQUESTS

WORRY WARTS

Give all your worries and cares to God, for he cares about you.
1 PETER 5:7 NLT

When we lived in the country, my husband bought a puppy. She was a black lab and St. Bernard mix—she had silky black hair and *really* big feet. I dubbed the puppy "Calamity."

One day, our family decided to go outside while Calamity took a nap. We initially took our jackets, but the weather was mild, so we ended up leaving them behind. Unfortunately, my daughter tossed hers onto a chair instead of hanging it on a hook.

If you've ever owned a puppy, you can probably tell where I'm going with this.

By the time we got home, tiny shreds of pink polar fleece covered the floor. I pulled the remains of the jacket out of Calamity's grasp. It had huge, gaping holes. It was missing several snaps. What was left of the coat was matted and chewed. My daughter dissolved into tears, and the guilty-looking pet was put into time-out. I added "new jacket" to the shopping list.

Worry is a vividly descriptive word. We tend to equate it with fear and anxiety, but we mustn't miss the subtle differences here. When you think of the word worry, think of a dog chewing up a pink polar fleece jacket.

You see, the dictionary definition of worry is "to shake or pull at with the teeth." Repeatedly pulling at, picking at, gnawing, tearing, chewing, and toying with something is worrying at it. When we go over and over concerns in our minds, worrying them continually, there can be no peace. Whether it's physical, mental, or emotional, worrying always creates a mess.

1. *The New Living Translation reads, "Neither our fears for today nor our worries about tomorrow—not even the powers of hell can separate us from God's love" (Romans 8:38). What do you see as the difference between fear and worry? What encouragement does this Scripture offer for both?*

2. *The secret fears we harbor in our hearts give rise to the worries that plague our minds. What is the result of worry on our mental and physical health? Solomon offers some words of wisdom in Proverbs 12:25. How might we focus on good words instead of our worries?*

3. *Our Savior knows about all our concerns, but He told His followers not to have "an anxious mind" (Luke 12:29 NKJV). In Matthew 6:25–34, Jesus says not to worry about tomorrow. Why not? What do you find reassuring about His message?*

4. *What kinds of things do you typically worry about? What worries would disappear for you if you concentrated solely on the day you are in?*

You may recall the story of Lazarus' two sisters, Mary and Martha (John 11:1). Jesus commended Mary for choosing that which was most important, while Martha was gently scolded by her Teacher for caring too much about supper preparations. "The Lord said to her, 'My dear Martha, you are worried and upset over all these details! There is only one thing worth being concerned about. Mary has discovered it, and it will not be taken away from her'" (Luke 10:41–42 NLT). But for many of us it's hard not to worry in the same way Martha did. We get caught up in the business of *this* day. So much to do, so many places to go, so many people to see. We know we shouldn't be worrying, but it comes so *naturally*! I'd encourage you to follow the Lord's advice, and don't worry about tomorrow—but remember not to worry too much over today either!

5. We have just one option when it comes to facing worry. Read Philippians 4:6. What does Paul say worriers should do?

6. Peter has the same idea Paul had about worry. Read 1 Peter 5:7. What are we told to do about our worries? How often do you actually put this into practice?

DIGGING DEEPER

Have you ever done a character study in the Bible? Now's your chance! Read everything recorded about these two very different sisters, Mary and Martha. They were dear friends of Jesus, and He was often a guest in their home. What can you learn about their personalities from these passages? What insights do you glean from them?

- Luke 10:38–42
- John 11
- John 12:1–8

PONDER & PRAY

Take a look around your heart and mind this week, and see if you find worries lurking where they do not belong. If you find more than you expected, start a list! When you have a concern that is plaguing your heart and occupying your mind, turn to the Lord who knows and loves you and surrender it in prayer. God can handle all of your worries; you don't need to carry the burden yourself. Once you relinquish it into His capable hands, you will discover peace.

ADDITIONAL NOTES & PRAYER REQUESTS

STRESSED OUT

My spirit is overwhelmed within me;
My heart within me is distressed.
PSALM 143:4 NKJV

"Your eyes were bigger than your stomach," my mother gently scolded as I brought her my half-filled plate. This was a frequent occurrence at the big family get-togethers in our home. Every few years, it would be our turn to host a get-together, and all our extended family would drive into town and crowd into our house. The meal was always potluck—my aunts were all good cooks and my uncles were all good eaters.

The buffet in our dining room would be lined with huge serving dishes of steaming food. The kids would get to go through the line first, and I would take liberally from all my favorite dishes. Only, with all the noise and excitement and chatter at the children's table, most of my food would go untouched. The dishes were gathered up and washed before dessert, so my uneaten food was always discovered, and that's when the scolding came. "Your eyes were bigger than your stomach."

Many of us scoop more onto our plates than we can handle in a day. It all looks good. A little more couldn't hurt. But pretty soon we realize our ambitions were bigger than our time. That's when stress begins to weigh us down. Do you have too much on your plate?

1. *Stress is defined as a state of mental or emotional strain resulting from demanding circumstances. In addition to the toll it takes on our emotional health, it can also lead to physical symptoms, including headaches, increased heart rate, muscle tension, and trouble sleeping. What words would you use to describe your emotions when you are under stress? What physical symptoms do you experience when you're stressed?*

2. Psalm 143:4 gives an apt description of the emotional turmoil within a stressed-out heart. What kinds of situations bring on these feelings in your day?

3. When we let ourselves get too busy, we pay for it with our ragged emotions. Do we really need to be as busy as we are? What does Psalm 39:6 say about busyness?

4. *There are times when we all feel the pressure; responsibilities start piling up, and stress sneaks into our lives. Read Psalm 102:1. Where should we turn when we are feeling overwhelmed?*

5. *Time is fleeting. So how do we use our time wisely? Look in Ephesians 5:15–16. I especially love the wording found in the New King James Version. What does "redeeming the time" mean to you?*

*My daugh*ter has long hair, perhaps because I never did. My mother grew weary of the wailing and tears that accompanied a good brushing. "It hurts," I'd cry. Eventually she set aside her comb and brought out the scissors.

So I have let my girl's hair grow out, and it is lovely—silky blonde waves that fall to her waist. We like to play with different styles, but we are in a daily battle against tangles. Tears well up in her eyes as I work the comb through a particularly tough spot, but I remind her that they will only get worse if we don't get rid of them.

Life is a little like that. When our schedules are tangled up, and there's no hope of straightening them out, it's time to make some changes. If we don't address the snarls early on, they will only get worse—until there's nothing left to do but bring out the scissors.

6. *As you face a tangle of responsibilities, and you feel the tension building in your heart, where can you turn to dispel the mounting levels of stress? There's a hint in Psalm 119:143.*

7. *Though these suggestions may help you survive the stresses of your day, it'd be nicer to get rid of the stress altogether! What kind of life do you long for? Write down your answer, then find Paul's recommendation in 1 Thessalonians 4:11.*

8. *When we fight through the noise and discover the quiet life, what will be the only busyness left to us? Check out the promise in Ecclesiastes 5:20.*

Digging Deeper

When days become flurries of activity and stress mounts, we long for a quiet haven of peace. The following verses speak of both a longing for peace and the promise of rest. In a group or by yourself, look at different translations of these Scriptures. How are both the verses and translations similar, and how are they different?

- Psalm 55:6
- Psalm 61:2
- Psalm 107:30
- Isaiah 14:7
- Zephaniah 3:17

Ponder & Pray

As we try to keep up with all that needs doing, stress can mount until we feel frantic. Instead of getting caught in a whirlpool of busyness that sucks you down into despair, ask God for the grace to face one task at a time. When stresses start to plague you, pray to Him for peace and a calm heart. Ask the Lord to lead you through your days, changing your spirit until it is quiet and gentle.

ADDITIONAL NOTES &
PRAYER REQUESTS

GOOD VENTILATION

I am praying to you because I know you will answer, O God.
Bend down and listen as I pray.
PSALM 17:6 NLT

Emotions are interesting things. We all have them, we all are affected by them, and we all try to hide them sometimes. But emotions don't like to stay hidden for long. In subtle, or not-so-subtle, ways, we broadcast our feelings to the world. Furrowed eyebrows, flaring nostrils, blushing cheeks, and pursed lips are physical tells that betray our inner thoughts. And then there are our words and actions.

We lose our temper. We have sleepless nights. We criticize ourselves and others. We complain, rant, and rage. We wallow in self-pity. We don't want to do these things. But our emotions need an outlet, and all too often they come rushing out in ways that feel beyond our control.

Unfortunately, none of these behaviors are appropriate for Christians. Proverbs 29:11 says, "A fool vents all his feelings, But a wise man holds them back" (NKJV). But that doesn't mean we should bottle it all up! God wants us to let go of our inner turbulence and find rest in Him.

1. *Who is someone you trust, someone who will listen with empathy and understanding—someone you can vent to? How has this person helped you?*

2. *Our Lord is even better than any earthly friend. He's available to us whenever we feel the need to unburden our hearts. David said, "Each morning I bring my requests to you and wait expectantly" (Psalm 5:3 NLT). What else does David say in Psalm 55:2?*

3. *When you are facing a tough day, how do you feel after you pray about it?*

4. *Read Jeremiah 29:12. What does God promise concerning our prayers?*

We all know someone who seems to complain about everything. Their constant venting can be downright depressing to listen to. Whenever one of our children starts whining and complaining, my husband interrupts the tirade and commands, "Put your eyebrows up." It might sound silly, but it works. It's *very* hard to maintain a frown while arching your eyebrows. Immediately, our child's expressions will dissolve into a smile and a giggle. Then they start to look at their problems with a new perspective.

When we're overwhelmed with negative emotions, the last thing we feel like doing is laughing about it. But when we learn to laugh at the little troubles that face us, we can shift us away from our negative thoughts and gain a whole new perspective. Don't let anger and resentment find a foothold in your heart. Instead, try to find the humor in the situation. Even the most frustrating event in your day can become a source of merriment if you keep a good sense of humor!

5. *Though it comes most naturally to let off steam in the form of angry words or bitter complaints, laughter is a wonderful alternative! Can you think of a frustrating experience you've had that could be turned into a funny story?*

6. *What does Solomon say about a sense of humor? Look at Proverbs 17:22.*

DIGGING DEEPER

In the midst of our fears, our worries, and our stresses, God encourages us to call for Him. No matter how we're feeling or what we're going through, He's always right there, waiting for us. Here are some verses to encourage you; all of them invite us to call on God. Which one speaks to you the most?

- Psalm 50:15
- Psalm 55:16–18
- Psalm 91:14–16
- Psalm 116:1–2
- Jeremiah 33:3

PONDER & PRAY

When your heart is troubled this week, or your fears and frustrations threaten to overwhelm you, turn to God. Pour it all out to Him and feel the relief of a good venting. He will lift those burdens right off your mind. This week, too, pray for God's strength to pray, smile, and even laugh in the midst of your emotional turmoil. Ask God to give you some perspective and to help you release your tensions with a hearty chuckle.

Additional Notes & Prayer Requests

BUILDING A FOUNDATION

Turn my eyes from worthless things,
And give me life through your word.
PSALM 119:37 NLT

When someone is wrapped up in their work, it can be difficult to get their attention. To compensate for this, we have established several means of polite interruption. A gentle clearing of the throat. A quiet "ahem" or "excuse me." A short little cough. All of these things signal to someone that you have entered their domain and would like to speak. We are taught to raise our hands for permission to speak in the classroom. In restaurants, we put on a hopeful look and try to catch the eye of our server. We let out a sharp whistle when hailing a cab or calling a dog. We use doorbells, countertop bells, car horns. We call, text, and email.

So how does God get our attention? We are busy people, and getting our attention can be a tricky business.

1. *Would you say you are really living, or just surviving? Do you find yourself longing for something quieter, less frenzied?*

2. *What has God used to catch your attention lately?*

3. *God resorts to outrageous means to get our attention sometimes. Moses needed a burning bush, and Jonah needed a whale. Is there a chance God is using stress to get your attention?*

My children love to build forts and castles with empty tissue boxes. When they were smaller (and we had fewer boxes) the walls of the fort were short and manageable. But as their coordination improved, their towers soared. They soon learned that in order to build a really tall tower, they needed to set the boxes on a table or hardwood floor. The carpeting had too much give, and the buildings would eventually come tumbling down.

Have you considered your foundations lately? Is your life teetering because it doesn't have a firm footing? As we work to build a more peaceful life for ourselves, we must first make sure that we have the right foundation.

4. *We are building our lives, too, and we must choose our foundation carefully. What does the parable in Matthew 7:24–27 teach us?*

5. *More advice about having a good foundation is found in 1 Timothy 6:19. Why does Paul say in this passage?*

6. *Let's back up a few verses. What does 1 Timothy 6:3 say is the foundation for a godly life?*

DIGGING DEEPER

Is God trying to capture your attention? It's far too easy for us to take God for granted during our busy days. When life becomes a whirlwind of activity and stress, we must scrutinize our foundations. Let's explore some verses of Scripture that address our foundation as Christians. Compare how different translations interpret the text. What picture do these verses paint, and what do you take away from it?

- Proverbs 10:25
- Isaiah 28:16
- 1 Corinthians 3:11
- 2 Timothy 2:19
- 1 Peter 5:10

Ponder & Pray

Has God been using a dissatisfaction with your hectic life to grab your attention? Pray for a clearness of understanding as you test your foundations. Have you built wisely? Do you need to renovate? Ask the Lord to guide you through the process of change that must come. Pray for assurance and peace that your choices are wise ones. He will give you joy as you build.

ADDITIONAL NOTES &
PRAYER REQUESTS

I KNOW WHOM I HAVE BELIEVED

As for me, I trust in You, O LORD;
I say, "You are my God."
PSALM 31:14 NKJV

D ating looks very different depending on how long a couple has been together. Think about it: when we're just beginning a new relationship, we want the other person to like us. We work hard to make a good impression. We get dressed up, we smile a lot, we laugh at all their jokes (even if they're not actually that funny). We present ourselves in the best possible light and learn as much as we can about our significant other.

But once we've been in a relationship for a while, we start to feel more secure. We relax. We see the other person when they don't look their best. When they're in a bad mood. When they're feeling discouraged. On the surface, it doesn't seem as romantic as the early stage of the relationship, but in reality each person is getting to know the other on a deeper level—they're working toward becoming *one*.

It's tricky to really get to know people. We hold back our true feelings because we don't know how someone will react. We guard our opinions to stay out of tiresome arguments. We tell people that we're fine because it's safer than admitting our hardships. And everybody else is doing it, too. With so much subterfuge going on, real friendships are slow to form. After all, how can you trust someone you do not know?

1. *Do you trust God with everything in your life? Or are there certain things you hold back from Him or try to handle on your own?*

2. *Have you ever been disappointed by somebody? Have you ever put your trust in someone only to have it betrayed? What does Psalm 118:8 caution?*

3. Why is it better to trust God? Psalm 9:10 gives a very good reason.

4. Look at Proverbs 3:5. When is it hardest for you to trust God? What circumstances have made it difficult for you to maintain your confidence in Him?

5. *If you believe in God's promises, how should that belief affect your everyday life? What about your fears? Worry? Stress?*

Did you like to play hide-and-seek when you were little? My sister and I loved it; one of us would squirm into a tiny corner, and the other would turn the house upside down trying to find her. It never really took long to find the hider, though. We would wiggle and giggle and peek out of our spot to see if the seeker was getting close. Hiding was great, but the real fun was in being found!

Have you ever felt like you were in a game of hide-and-seek with God? There are times in our lives when we feel like God has hidden Himself from us. We feel so very alone, and we long to find Him again. In the Bible, God often welcomes us to seek after Him. And He wants to be found, too! God has promised that if we seek Him, we will find Him!

6. *We have already stated that it's hard to trust someone you don't truly know. So how do you get to know God? What does Jeremiah 29:13 promise?*

7. *Read 2 Samuel 22:31. How has God proven Himself to you?*

8. *Trusting God has its benefits. When we are secure in the knowledge of His love and care, we are not easily shaken by our circumstances. But there is another wonderful result of our confidence in God. What does David say about this in Psalm 73:28?*

_____

_____

_____

_____

_____

_____

DIGGING DEEPER

God promises much to those who trust in Him. If you believe what He says is true, then take the leap of faith to live that way. Here are several verses that deal with trusting God. Allow them to strengthen your confidence in your Savior.

- Psalm 9:10
- Psalm 18:2
- Psalm 34:22
- Psalm 37:5
- Nahum 1:7

PONDER & PRAY

If God seems to be hiding from you lately, take this next week to earnestly seek Him. What joy you will have when you find Him! As you study His Word and get to know Him more, pray that He will help you to trust Him. Release into His hands all the little cares and worries that plague your day. He will prove Himself to be faithful in every detail.

Additional Notes & Prayer Requests

A Promise Is a Promise

Let us hold tightly without wavering to the hope we affirm, for God can be trusted to keep his promise.
HEBREWS 10:23 NLT

We can tell a lot about a person by the promises they make and how well they keep them. For example, we all know someone who's bad at keeping their word. They flake out on plans, miss deadlines, arrive late to events. They may be a nice person, and you might enjoy spending time with them, but you don't have a lot of faith in them when they promise to do something.

On the other hand, you probably know someone who consistently does what they say they'll do. They make promises that they know they can follow through on, and then they fulfill those promises. We consider that person as responsible, someone with integrity. We know we can trust them.

In order to better manage our anxiety and stress, we need to connect with God on a deeper level. One of the best ways to get to know God is to seek Him out through His Word. He has made many promises to us, but we can't discover what they are until we open our Bibles. We all know how much it can hurt when the people in our lives break their promises to us, but we never have to have that fear with God. Everything He has promised will come to be. We can put our trust in Him, especially when the going gets tough. This session is dedicated to exploring just a few of God's precious promises.

1. *As we seek a deeper relationship with God, let's keep in mind the promise Jesus makes in Matthew 7:7–8. What does He make a point of saying?*

2. We know that we can pray to God about the things that are troubling us. But when we repeatedly pray about something and nothing seems to change, we start to wonder if God is really listening to us. What does David say about this in Psalm 66:19?

3. Not only does God always hear us, but He also sees everything we do. What are we assured of in Hebrews 6:10–11?

4. *When we're feeling overwhelmed by anxiety or stress, it can feel like we're simply not strong enough to keep going. What does Paul have to say about this in 2 Corinthians 12:9–10?*

5. *God will stay with us through our hardships, but more than that, He also promises to give us peace of mind. Check out Isaiah 26:3.*

6. Is God only there for us when we feel like we need Him? Of course not! God loves us each and every day of our lives. Read Isaiah 46:4.

7. God's promises extend far beyond what we can imagine. What is His ultimate gift to us, according to 1 Peter 1:3–5?

DIGGING DEEPER

One of the most wonderful promises God has made to us is that He will be with us through all our trials and tribulations. When we're anxious or stressed, it's easy to feel alone, like no one understands. But God sees everything, and He is always with us. We can depend on Him to help us through the hard times. We see this promise again and again in the Scriptures. Below are just a few examples. Take some time to meditate on these, and make a list of your own favorite promises and blessings in the additional notes section at the end of this session.

- Psalm 55:22
- Isaiah 41:13
- Isaiah 43:2
- Isaiah 54:10
- Joshua 1:9

PONDER & PRAY

This week, as you pore over God's Word and seek Him in prayer, ask the Lord to show you His promises, and ask Him to strengthen your faith in Him. Choose a few promises that speak to your deepest needs and repeat them to yourself often. Commit them to memory and speak them aloud with confidence. God will keep His word.

Additional Notes & Prayer Requests

Two Little Letters

> *"Let your 'Yes' be 'Yes,' and your 'No,' 'No.'"*
> MATTHEW 5:37 NKJV

When I was a new mom, my husband and I rented a small apartment just up the hill from the seminary he was attending. While he tackled ancient languages, systematic theology, and principles of church growth, I tackled piles of laundry, dirty dishes, and soiled diapers. He was weighed down with a full course load and working as many hours as he could to make ends meet. Then came the perfect opportunity for us to earn some extra money. One of my husband's fellow seminary students was also a new daddy, and his wife was back to working full-time. Could I watch his little boy while he was in class?

What could be better? The child would be dropped off every morning and picked back up in under two hours. I could earn a little extra money, and I was doing the parents a great favor. I agreed, and on Monday morning, an eight-month-old Caleb was deposited in our living room. He came equipped with a playpen and a diaper bag the size of a steamer trunk. His father instructed me on his usual routine, his likes and his dislikes.

What he didn't tell me was that Caleb was a screamer.

The moment his father left, Caleb sent up a piercing wail that did not stop. I rocked him, fed him, sang to him, checked his diaper—nothing worked. Poor Caleb was inconsolable. I was a brand-new mom; I had no idea how to help him. In the end, I set the shrieking child in his playpen and took my own baby into our bedroom. I let him cry.

You'd think it would have gotten better over time, but Caleb never warmed to his early morning visits. For the rest of the semester, he would scream for a solid hour. And all the while I lay on my bed in the other room, wishing I had never agreed to babysit. Since then I have learned to consider much more carefully before I say "yes" to something.

As we work to design a calmer, happier life for ourselves, let's take some time to analyze our commitments carefully. Do you have too much on your plate? Is there something you do regularly that you dread? Are there commitments you could pass off to someone else? Even a small commitment can cause a lot of emotional strain if we don't guard our time carefully.

1. *Do you have trouble saying no? What makes it so hard to turn people down?*

2. *Is it wise to say yes to everything that comes your way? Of course not! Paul gives Christians some good advice in Ephesians 5:15. What is it?*

3. *From the Bible, we know God has a plan for us and a purpose in everything that happens to us. God is at work in our lives, but why? Check out Philippians 2:13.*

4. *You have been seeking God and establishing your trust in Him. Have you also consulted with God about His will and your plans? Look at Deuteronomy 10:12. What does God want you to do?*

As a child, I was a fussy eater, picking and choosing my way through a meal. Some kids use their forks like a shovel, but mine was a finely tuned instrument for dissecting casseroles. From the depths of a dish concocted of hamburger, cheese, and noodles, I dug up the tiny squares of mushrooms and lined them up on the edge of my plate.

Christians need to be picky, too. We can't just shovel in everything the world dishes up. Sure, a lot of it is good stuff, but let's not be hasty! God warns us to be circumspect. He wants us to assess our opportunities carefully and be selective about what we choose. If God is leading you into something new, He will give you both the peace to accept it and the strength to accomplish it!

5. Our wisest course of action in this busy world is to keep our focus and say no to anything that does not help us toward our ultimate goal. Do you have goals? What are they?

6. When we learn to say no to things, we suddenly have time to catch our breath, to think, to rest in the Lord, and to pray. What one thing would you choose to do if you knew you had a week full of quiet evenings ahead of you?

7. Once you have taken the time to rest and recharge, you start to feel like you could take on more. In your self-confidence, it's easy to start saying yes again before seeking God's will in some new venture. What does James 4:15 say about this?

8. Saying no can be tough, but you need to hang in there! God will bless your efforts to pursue His perfect path. What promise are we given in Hebrews 10:36?

DIGGING DEEPER

In our hearts, we long to hear the words, "Well done, good and faithful servant." We want to please and glorify God. We want to do His will. So what is God's will? Several Scriptures give us a glimpse. Let's explore them and consider how we might apply the principles in our own lives. You can use the section at the end of this session to take notes. Discuss your ideas with a small group if you belong to one.

- 1 Thessalonians 5:14–18
- 1 Peter 2:15–17
- 1 Peter 4:2, 7–11
- 1 John 5:1–4, 14

PONDER & PRAY

This week, ask the Lord to help you see your life with new clarity. Are there opportunities to which you should begin saying no? Pray for discernment so you can tell the difference between things that are merely *good* and those that are *best*. Pray for a new focus and the ability to decide if the things that come your way will work towards your goals or against them. Guard your time this week and treat it as precious. Then, when God gives you an avenue of service, do that thing with all your heart!

Additional Notes & Prayer Requests

SETTING THE PACE

You also aspire to lead a quiet life, to mind your own business,
and to work with your own hands, as we commanded you.
1 THESSALONIANS 4:11 NKJV

There's nothing like the good old days, or so we're told. But gone are the days of the wall-mounted telephone and dial-up modem. Now we have smartphones and virtual assistants that can do just about anything for us, and the technology keeps advancing. Things are noisier now, with so many apps, games, podcasts, news outlets, websites, and streaming services clamoring for our attention. And in the midst of all this hubbub, we come across this ancient verse of Scripture that says, "Aspire to lead a quiet life."

What are we supposed to do with that? Do we need to pack up our families, move out into the distant hills, and live on homegrown vegetables and goat's milk for the rest of our lives? Of course not. Quiet lives are not defined by quiet surroundings; they're defined by a quiet and gentle spirit. But what exactly does that *mean*, and how can we cultivate that in our lives?

1. *The dictionary defines "quiet" as being calm, untroubled, and free of turmoil and agitation. How would you compare this sort of attitude to a life plagued by anxiety and stress?*

2. *What is currently robbing the quiet from your life? Is it a situation, maybe even a particular person? How do you think you might start cultivating a quiet life in spite of this?*

3. *Setting the pace of our life has a lot to do with adjusting our attitudes, so let's talk about complaining. James 5:9 says, "Do not grumble against one another, brethren, lest you be condemned" (NKJV). Paul gives us a better pattern to follow when we feel like complaining. What do Ephesians 4:2–3 and Colossians 3:13 tell us to do instead?*

Sometimes, the Christian life involves a lot of hard work, but there are always times of quiet rest for each of us. Have you ever been to the performance of a large symphony orchestra? In the beginning, as you find your seat and browse through the program, the members of the orchestra begin to slip into their seats. One by one, the musicians tuning their instruments and warming up. It sounds like a jumbled nonsense. Then the conductor arrives. All eyes turn to him as he raises his baton. The music begins, every instrument doing its part, and now the sound isn't jumbled at all. It is beautiful and breathtaking.

If you watch the orchestra pit carefully, you notice something. Though every seat is filled, not all the musicians are playing at every moment. As the conductor leads them through the music, some sections play, while others are at rest. When greater sound is called for, many are busy. When a soft movement is underway, a single instrument may have the spotlight. Yet all the orchestra members keep their eye on the conductor's baton.

The church is like that orchestra. We all keep our eyes on the Conductor, awaiting His direction. At times, we work hard, and the music of our lives is glorious. At other times, we are allowed to rest. Others take up the song. Life has that sort of ebb and flow. Whether you are giving your all right now, or are in a season of attentive rest, quietly waiting your turn, you are an important part of a larger group. And the result of our interwoven lives is beautiful, a perfect harmony glorifying God.

4. *Let's take another look at 1 Thessalonians 4:11. In addition to leading a quiet life, Paul also encourages Christians to mind their own business. Why do you think that is important within the church? Aren't we supposed to be caring for one another?*

5. *Does Paul's advice mean we should avoid contact with one another? Of course not! Have you ever noticed that many of the commands we are given in the Bible and many of the gifts and talents we receive from the Holy Spirit are only useful in group settings? What does 1 Peter 4:10 say?*

6. *We Christians are to be working together in harmony, creating a beautiful example of love and unity. Ephesians 4:32 says, "Be kind to one another, tenderhearted, forgiving one another, just as God in Christ forgave you" (NKJV). We are a part of a caring community. What does Hebrews 10:24 encourage us to do?*

7. *We are supposed to live a quiet life, but we are not to become hermits, burying our talents in the ground. At the same time, we are to show caring concern for our fellow Christians, but we are not to become busybodies and meddlers. In setting the pace for your life, which of these paths comes more naturally to you? What can you do to keep a balance between the two?*

DIGGING DEEPER

As we get to work building quieter lives and placing our anxiety and stress into God's capable hands, we cannot forget one another or our place in the community. In fact, focusing less on ourselves and more on other people can be an effective way to cultivate a quiet and gentle mindset. The Bible is filled with passages that encourage Christians to love and care for one another. Read the following Scriptures and think about how you can live out these commandments.

- John 13:34–35
- Romans 12:10
- Galatians 6:2
- 1 Thessalonians 5:11
- 1 Peter 4:8–10

PONDER & PRAY

Pray this week for a quiet life—one unbothered by worries or caught up in busyness. Stifle the urge to gossip or complain. Ask the Lord to help you pursue His will each day with a quiet and gentle spirit. Then ask Him to show you ways to touch others who are looking harried and haggard. It doesn't take much to give a friend a little lift! Encourage one another this week.

ADDITIONAL NOTES &
PRAYER REQUESTS

STEADY AS SHE GOES

Not that I have already attained, or am already
perfected; but I press on, that I may lay hold of that
for which Christ Jesus has also laid hold of me.
PHILIPPIANS 3:12 NKJV

Growing up, my family lived in a farming community, and farm cats were plentiful, with a new litter arriving every spring. My mother was not fond of these critters—or vultures, as she called them. Rabbits would have been a better comparison, considering how much they multiplied. At one point, we had more than twenty cats. Every day they would drape themselves across our front step, sunning themselves and waiting for table scraps. Mom declared that enough was enough. We could keep a few tomcats for mousing, but the rest would have to go.

We gave away free kittens. We donated several adult cats to the surrounding farms. The front step was cleared. Mom was pleased. Then, Peaches came back. Peaches was a particularly fruitful mama kitty, known to give both spring and fall litters. She'd walked home from the farm where she'd been dropped off—five miles away. It was amazing! Such devotion! Such determination!

But Mom was adamant. She would have to go back. This time, Dad called a farmer who lived ten miles away. Peaches was accepted into a new barn on a dairy farm. But two weeks later, she was back. We were astonished. We were amused. Well, everyone besides Mom.

In the end, we had to take Peaches to a farm on the other side of a wide river to keep her from returning. She settled down there and blessed that farm with many a litter of orange kittens.

Sometimes our worries are like that. We pray. We repent. We set those worries at God's feet and walk away, only to find them back on our doorstep the next day. Though we give up our anxieties and stresses, they slowly make their way back to us, surprising us with their presence after long weeks of absence. What do we do when fears and worries start to worm their way back into our lives?

1. *We all want to move forward in our Christian walk, making steady progress on a smooth path. But sometimes the hill is steep, and our footing begins to slip. Do you sometimes feel like you're taking two steps forward, and one step back? What do you do in these situations?*

2. When our prayers go unanswered, or our worst fears are realized, one of our first reactions is to ask, "Doesn't God love me anymore?" or "Am I a bad Christian?" What does 1 Peter 1:6–7 say about these trials we face?

3. Whether you stumble over some rock in the road or trip over your own shoelaces, keep on walking. Don't give up! Have patience in the process. What does James 1:2–4 encourage us to do?

4.   *When a huge crisis comes into our lives, we often find the gumption to face it bravely and with grace. However, when a bunch of little things go wrong in our day, we've met our match. Do you have trouble maintaining your calm in the face of daily setbacks, misunderstandings, conflicts, and messes? What do you do when this happens?*

5.   *Paul says "everything else is worthless when compared with the infinite value of knowing Christ Jesus my Lord" (Philippians 3:8 NLT). That's the biblical way of saying, "Don't sweat the small stuff!" What does 1 John 5:4–5 declare?*

Most of our days are filled with tasks we have to redo again and again. We wash the same dishes we just washed the day before. We launder the same clothes over and over. We re-vacuum rooms. We re-mow the lawn. We re-wash our hair and re-brush our teeth. Sometimes we wish the things we did would just stay done!

These same kinds of maintenance issues come into play in our spiritual lives. We must reread the Scriptures over and over. We must confess our sins to the Lord on a regular basis. And just when we think we have given all of our cares over to God, we find them sneaking back. That's part of being human.

Don't be surprised if you have to deal with your fears and frustrations more than once. But don't feel defeated, as if you didn't get it right the first time. Anxiety and stress may pop up from time to time, but as we continue to build our lives in Christ, it'll be easier to let go and let God.

6. *When it comes right down to it, there is only one way to get to know God enough to trust Him. There is only one way to deepen our relationship with Him. There is only one way we can know how to please God. There is only one place we can turn to hear His voice. What does Jesus say about this is in John 8:31?*

7. *When we have an abiding faith in God, we are assured victorious lives. How would you define victory? What does Revelation 21:7 say?*

DIGGING DEEPER

When our anxiety and stress come creeping back, it's easy to get discouraged. But we have to hang in there and depend upon God. He promises great things to those who are able to overcome. The book of Revelation holds several such promises. Discuss with your group or ponder on your own what these promises may look like.

- Revelation 2:7
- Revelation 2:17
- Revelation 2:26
- Revelation 3:5
- Revelation 3:12
- Revelation 3:21

PONDER & PRAY

Make yourself the subject of study this week. Notice what pushes your buttons or leads to anxious thoughts. Ask the Lord to help you understand yourself better. Then pray for the Spirit to intervene when you feel your stress begin to spike. Depend on His strength to calm your fears and cool your anger. Abide in His Word this week, and abide in Jesus. Pray for a new perspective, a changed attitude, and a transformed heart.

Additional Notes & Prayer Requests

PERFECT PEACE

"Peace I leave with you, My peace I give to you;
not as the world gives do I give to you. Let not your
heart be troubled, neither let it be afraid."

JOHN 14:27 NKJV

Of all God's gifts to His believers, peace has proven the most difficult for the enemy to counterfeit. Lust can masquerade as love. Pride can hide in a cloak of humility or generosity. Temporary happiness will often look more appealing than true joy. But when it comes to peace, you either have it or you don't.

What is peace? We all know what peace should feel like, even if it has been a while since we've experienced it for ourselves. We sing about peace in our worship services. We say to each other, "Peace be with you." We strive both for world peace and for our own personal peace of mind. All of us long for the calmness, serenity, and quiet confidence that comes from a truly peaceful heart.

Peace is a little foretaste of heaven, and God gives it to us freely. But we have to decide to accept it and bring it into our lives. The gift of peace is ours, and the Scriptures say we should let it rule in our hearts. In this final session, let's explore how to do exactly that.

1. *Paul promises that the God of peace will be with us whenever we do . . . what? Read Philippians 4:8–9.*

2. *Does peace mean freedom from conflict? Unfortunately, no. But what does Jesus tell us in John 16:33?*

3. *What does Colossians 3:15 have to say about peace?*

4. *Philippians 4:6–7 is an often-quoted passage on the subject of peace. What insights do you glean from it?*

5. *So how do we bring peace into our lives? Do we just sit back and let the Lord pour it over us? Well, yes and no. What do Romans 14:19 and 1 Peter 3:11 urge us to do?*

6. *Pursuing peace in our own lives is a worthy goal, but as Christians we are also expected to extend peace to others. 1 Thessalonians 5:13 and Hebrews 12:14 describe the peace that should exist between one another.*

DIGGING DEEPER

The Father, the Son, and the Holy Spirit all offer to bring us peace into our lives. Let's look at some Scriptures that connect the three parts of the Trinity to peace. If you own multiple translations or are part of a group, look at how the wording and meaning can change depending on the translation. What new insights do you gain from these passages? Use the additional notes section at the end of this session to meditate on them.

- 2 Corinthians 13:11
- Romans 5:1
- Isaiah 9:6
- Ephesians 2:14
- Galatians 5:22
- Romans 15:13

PONDER & PRAY

God has asked you to trust Him. He has told you not to worry. He has promised you peace. Though your life may be in a state of turmoil that makes the idea of peace seem ridiculous, remember God has promised us a peace that surpasses understanding. This week, as you ponder these Scriptures, pray for His gift of everlasting peace, and let it rule in your heart!

Additional Notes & Prayer Requests

LEADER'S GUIDE

SESSION 1

1. Between our regular responsibilities at work, at home, at church, in our family, in our friend groups, and in our communities, it's no wonder our days fill up fast! If you're part of a group study and feel comfortable, share your list with your group members. Look at the similarities and differences between your lists.

2. If you're feeling overwhelmed by all your responsibilities, take a look at your list and see if there's something you could step away from, even if just for a little while. It's okay to set some things aside in order to cultivate some quiet space for yourself.

3. When it comes to important things, many of us would begin with the people who are closest to us. But God has also given us special passions and hobbies that we need to make time for as well—His gifts lend richness to our lives. Sometimes when our days get too busy, it can be difficult to prioritize the things that are most important to us, which causes even more stress in our lives. If there is something important to you that doesn't appear on your list of responsibilities—of things you regularly make time for—find a way to prioritize it.

4. "'For I know the plans I have for you,' says the LORD. 'They are plans for good and not for disaster, to give you a future and a hope. In those days when you pray, I will listen. If you look for me wholeheartedly, you will find me. I will be found by you,' says the LORD. 'I will end your captivity and restore your fortunes. I will gather you out of

the nations where I sent you and will bring you home again to your own land'" (Jeremiah 29:11–14 NLT). God has such wonderful plans for our lives! Whenever we're low on hope, we can turn to Him in prayer, and He will hear us. He will stay with us through the storm, and He will restore our peace and prosperity. He will help us find the comforting, happy home we are looking for.

5. "A prayer of one overwhelmed with trouble, pouring out problems before the Lord. Lord, hear my prayer! Listen to my plea! Don't turn away from me in my time of distress. Bend down your ear and answer me quickly when I call to you, for my days disappear like smoke" (Psalm 102:1–3 NLT). Some of my days certainly do seem to disappear like smoke! When David feels overwhelmed and distressed in the face of his problems, he turns to the Lord to pour out his troubles.

6. In the midst of all our activities and responsibilities, we can lose sight of the fact that God made us the way we are for a purpose. We are His workmanship—The New Living Translation calls us God's "masterpiece." Ephesians 2:10 reminds us that we are created for good works, and if we concentrate on doing good in our homes and our communities, we will glorify our Creator.

SESSION 2

1. "You shall not be afraid of the terror by night" (Psalm 91:5 NKJV). "When you lie down, you will not be afraid; yes, you will lie down and your sleep shall be sweet" (Proverbs 3:24 NKJV). Still, many of us spend too many hours of the night tossing and turning instead of getting our rest. When fears come creeping in after dark and wakeful nights come, turn them into sweet hours of prayer, and soon you'll find peace and rest.

2. The psalmist declares "They won't be afraid of bad news; their hearts are steady because they trust the LORD" (Psalm 112:7 NCV). When we put our faith and trust in God, He can dispel all our fears.

3. "Don't be afraid of the evil things people say, and don't be upset by their insults" (Isaiah 51:7 NCV). The New Living Translation calls such insults "people's scorn" and "slanderous talk." Pay no attention to the gossip that is flung about. Don't be afraid of what people might say, so long as you are walking in a way that pleases God.

4. Jesus says, "I say to you, My friends, do not be afraid of those who kill the body" (Luke 12:4 NKJV). And why is that? Because once you are dead, you are beyond their reach. Paul never dreaded death, for he said, "For me, to live is Christ, and to die is gain" (Philippians 1:21 NKJV).

5. "Do not be afraid; only believe" (Mark 5:36 NKJV). In the face of every doubt and fear, God asks us to put our trust in Him. Nothing is impossible for Him (Luke 1:37), and He cares about what happens to you (1 Peter 5:7).

6. "Two sparrows cost only a penny, but not even one of them can die without your Father's knowing it. God even knows how many hairs are on your head. So don't be afraid. You are worth much more than many sparrows" (Matthew 10:29–31 NCV). You are precious to God. Though you may be facing uncertain times, don't allow your fears to overwhelm the truth of God's sovereign love.

7. "God has come to save me. I will trust in him and not be afraid. The LORD GOD is my strength and my song; he has become my salvation" (Isaiah 12:2 NLT). God has saved you—you are His, and safe for all eternity. He will give you the strength you need for the day you are facing. Not only that, God will give you a song—joy in the midst of everyday living.

8. I love the term of endearment here: "Do not fear, little flock, for it is your Father's good pleasure to give you the kingdom" (Luke 12:32 NKJV). Consider what God has in store for us when we reach eternity. It helps to put our fears here on earth in perspective!

SESSION 3

1. Fear can prevent us from living our lives because of what might happen, but worry allows that dread to spill over into all our tomorrows. Our worries are spawned by the fears we harbor in our hearts. But God's love always surrounds us, no matter what we're experiencing.

2. Psalm 37:8 declares, "Do not fret—it only causes harm" (NKJV). Constant worry can lead to headaches, stomachaches, ulcers, even mental illnesses like anxiety and depression. Living in a constant state of apprehension is just not good for us! Solomon says, "Worry weighs a person down; an encouraging word cheers a person up" (Proverbs 12:25 NLT). Try to focus more on positive things throughout the day, especially when you feel worry and dread creeping in. Keeping a gratitude journal or reminding yourself of God's promises can be a great way to refocus your thoughts.

3. "Do not worry about tomorrow, for tomorrow will worry about its own things. Sufficient for the day is its own trouble" (Matthew 6:34 NKJV). Every day is full enough. We certainly don't need to borrow trouble from tomorrow. When we concentrate on what is before us, we get less overwhelmed by future responsibilities.

4. There's never a shortage of things to worry about! We might worry about making a mistake at our job, forgetting something important, making ends meet, getting somewhere on time. All of us at least occasionally worry about our health, our finances, our families, and

our future. And not a bit of the worrying does any good. If we narrow our focus to the here and now and do what we can, many of those issues will resolve themselves in time.

5. "Don't worry about anything; instead pray about everything. Tell God what you need, and thank Him for all He has done" (Philippians 4:6 NLT). If you find your mind spinning, and worries consuming your thoughts, pray! Talk to God about the concerns that are nagging at you. Then count your blessings. Remind yourself of how He has taken care of everything in the past. Your worries will slip away.

6. "Give all your worries and cares to God, for He cares about you" (1 Peter 5:7 NLT). Even if it is something small, and seemingly insignificant in the face of eternity, God cares about it because He loves you. Make it a habit to put your worries into His hands, and He'll take care of them for you.

SESSION 4

1. Stress affects all of us differently, depending on our personality style. It can weigh us down so that we're gloomy, despondent, and withdrawn. It can get us all worked up, so that we're flying around trying to do three things at once, never stopping to take a breath. Some of us try to hide from our problems. Some of us feel like crying, others like shouting. Many of us find ourselves on an emotional roller coaster, feeling all of the above. In addition to the physical symptoms mentioned in the question, if left unchecked, stress can lead to depression, anxiety, and panic attacks.

2. David cries out "My spirit is overwhelmed within me; My heart within me is distressed" (Psalm 143:4 NKJV). The New Living Translation puts the same verse this way: "I am losing all hope; I am paralyzed with fear." It doesn't always take much to bring on these feelings. Sometimes even everyday occurrences—such as looming deadlines, noisy children, financial burdens, a messy house—can be enough to plunge us into despair.

3. "All our busy rushing ends in nothing" (Psalm 39:6 NLT). Our busyness doesn't do us any good if it causes us to miss the really important things in life. Our days really are few on this earth, and we need to consider very carefully how we will use them.

4. "A prayer of one overwhelmed with trouble, pouring out problems before the LORD. LORD, hear my prayer! Listen to my plea" (Psalm 102:1 NLT). God is our only help in these circumstances! He will always listen to us if we turn to Him.

5. "See then that you walk circumspectly, not as fools but as wise, redeeming the time" (Ephesians 5:15–16 NKJV). The New Century Version puts it this way: "Use every chance you have for doing good." Put simply, Paul asks that we make the most of our time on earth. Think of "redeeming the time" as investing your time in the things that really matter. As Christians we are expected to manage our time wisely and use every opportunity to worship and glorify God.

6. "As pressure and stress bear down on me, I find joy in your commands" (Psalm 119:143 NLT). Though your day might be packed with tasks, if you carve out some time to spend with the Lord, you will discover a wellspring of peace. Reading His Word will smooth your ruffled feathers and quiet your overworked mind.

7. Paul says, "Aspire to lead a quiet life to mind your own business, and to work with your own hands" (1 Thessalonians 4:11 NKJV). Is that similar to what you wrote down? We'll discuss what exactly a quiet life *is* and how to achieve it in session 10.

8. "God keeps such people so busy enjoying life that they take no time to brood over the past" (Ecclesiastes 5:20 NCV). I don't know about you, but I'd love to trade in my stress for the busyness of enjoying life!

SESSION 5

1. It's important to have a true friend whom you can fully confide in. Someone who cares about you, listens without judging, and encourages you to leave the frustrations behind once they've been voiced.

2. "Please listen and answer me, for I am overwhelmed by my troubles" (Psalm 55:2 NLT). When we are feeling overwhelmed, God will listen to us vent. He will listen to what we dare not tell another soul.

3. It never ceases to amaze me how prayer can transform. When we turn to God with a troubled heart, He is able to help us with our tangled emotions. Our anger is defused, our fears are calmed, our confusion is replaced by understanding, our broken heart is soothed, and our jealousy ebbs away. When our first reaction to frustration and dismay is to turn to God, He meets us and gives us immediate support.

4. "You will call my name. You will come to me and pray to Me, and I will listen to you" (Jeremiah 29:12 NCV). When we go looking for God, He allows us to find Him. God is listening. He hears our prayers. And He promises to answer us.

5. Have you ever noticed how often stand-up comedians tell stories about their embarrassing moments, misunderstandings, huge mistakes, and big messes? The next time you feel frustrated, try saying to

yourself, "This will make a great story!" Laughing over your troubles can take the sting out of them.

6. "A cheerful heart is good medicine" (Proverbs 17:22 NLT). Sometimes the best thing we can do to relieve our tension is to have a good laugh. Do whatever it takes: watch a comedy, read a funny book, plan a game night. Laughter can be wonderful medicine for whatever is plaguing you. And the best part is, when we choose to release some of our frustrations with laughter, we allow others around us to relax and join in the fun!

SESSION 6

1. Are you rushing through your days, flitting from one thing to another, but never settling down to finish anything? Do you rush into work in the morning to avoid the mess at home, then rush home in the evening, glad to be rid of your job for another day? If you are always running away from something, you are probably just surviving. If you find yourself feeling restless and longing for peace, don't despair. God can use a feeling of restlessness in our spirits to prepare us for something new ahead. It's time to take some practical steps toward a more peaceful and contented life.

2. God uses so many things to arrest our attention: the words of a friend or spouse, a comment from a stranger, the actions of our children. He uses the books we read, the TV shows we watch, the radio stations we listen to, even the magazine we browse through at the doctor's office. Then there's our pastor's sermon, our Sunday school classes, our Bible study group. Most of all, God uses His Word and the Spirit to nudge us in the right direction.

3. If God is using stress to get your attention, it's because He has something better planned for you. So your crazy life might just be a blessing in disguise. But that doesn't mean you should stay crazy! God is giving you the chance to take a long, careful look at your life. He wants to take your current crisis and turn it into a turning point.

4. Jesus uses the same illustration in Luke's Gospel: "He is like a man building a house, who dug deep and laid the foundation on the rock" (Luke 6:48 NKJV). We are to be like that wise builder, digging deep and creating a solid foundation for our days. Only then will we be unshakeable when the storms and floods beat against us.

5. The New Living Translation puts it this way: "They will be storing up their treasure as a good foundation for the future so that they may take hold of real life" (1 Timothy 6:19). In this case, "real life" means our eternal life. The choices we make now will echo on into eternity. Our day-to-day troubles start to feel a little flimsy when we're considering the whole of eternity!

6. "These are the sound, wholesome teachings of the Lord Jesus Christ. These teachings promote a godly life" (1 Timothy 6:3 NLT). Getting organized is always a good thing, but don't try to reshape your life without God. Whatever you build on your own strength is bound to fail. Don't neglect your relationship with your Lord. Soak yourself in His "sound, wholesome teachings" and in prayer. He will help you build a transformed life!

SESSION 7

1. Somehow, it's easier to trust God with our eternal souls than it is to trust Him with the little everyday details of our lives. We tend to let Him handle the "big stuff" and try to cover all the "little stuff" on our own strength. Unfortunately, that can lead to a life of worry and stress. God has told us over and over that He cares about the smallest of details, even the lives of the sparrows and the number of hairs on our head. We can trust Him, because He already knows us completely!

2. "It is better to trust in the LORD Than to put confidence in man" (Psalm 118:8 NKJV). People are not perfect, and disappointments are inevitable. But God will never lie to us or let us down. We can place our full confidence in Him.

3. "Those who know the LORD trust him, because he will not leave those who come to him" (Psalm 9:10 NCV). God will never forsake His own. We can depend upon Him. He will never betray our trust.

4. All of us have unique experiences, but most of us would probably agree that we have the hardest time trusting God when we can't understand what He's doing. When we depend on our own understanding, we become confused.

5. If you really trust God, then your life can be transformed by His promises to you. When He says you don't have to fear, you can rejoice and release your fear and trembling. When He says not to worry about tomorrow, you are blessed with the chance to concentrate on the day you are in. When you really believe God's promises will come to pass and live that way, your life will be changed forever.

6. "You will seek Me and find Me, when you search for Me with all your heart" (Jeremiah 29:13 NKJV). God is just waiting for us to seek Him out. He wants us to pursue Him. When we seek Him out, He will make Himself known to us.

7. "As for God, His way is perfect; The word of the LORD is proven; He is a shield to all who trust in Him" (2 Samuel 22:31 NKJV). If you look for them, you can probably find examples of God's promises being fulfilled in your own life. The more you get to know Him, the more you'll be able to see the ways in which He has proven Himself to you.

8. "As for me, how good it is to be near God! I have made the Sovereign LORD my shelter, and I will tell everyone about the wonderful things you do" (Psalm 73:28 NLT). As our relationship with God is strengthened by our trust, we have great opportunities to tell others about God's faithfulness. When God is good, don't hesitate to proclaim it. It will encourage your fellow believers, and it will draw the interest and attention of those who are still seeking Him.

SESSION 8

1. "Ask, and it will be given to you; seek, and you will find; knock, and it will be opened to you. For everyone who asks receives, and he who seeks finds, and to him who knocks it will be opened" (Matthew 7:7–8). If we look for God, He assures us that we will find Him. He wants us to seek Him out! God loves us, and He will give us good things if we have enough faith to ask for them.

2. "But certainly God has heard me; He has attended to the voice of my prayer. Blessed be God, Who has not turned away my prayer, Nor His mercy from me!" (Psalm 66:19–20). Even if it seems like He isn't answering them, God always pays attention to our prayers. You can rest in the promise that He will attend to your needs, for His mercy and grace are everlasting.

3. "God is not unjust to forget your work and labor of love which you have shown toward His name, in that you have ministered to the saints, and do minister. And we desire that each one of you show the same diligence to the full assurance of hope until the end" (Hebrews 6:10–11). Sometimes doing the right thing can seem like a thankless job, but God sees, knows, and will remember all the work you have done for Him. You can put your faith and your hope in Him and know that He will reward you in eternity.

4. "He said to me, "My grace is sufficient for you, for My strength is made perfect in weakness." Therefore most gladly I will rather boast in my infirmities, that the power of Christ may rest upon me. Therefore I take pleasure in infirmities, in reproaches, in needs, in persecutions, in distresses, for Christ's sake. For when I am weak, then I am strong" (2 Corinthians 12:9–10). We don't have to be strong or perfect. God has given us the gift of His grace, and He will use our imperfections and our weaknesses to highlight His own power and glory.

5. "You will keep him in perfect peace, Whose mind is stayed on You, Because he trusts in You" (Isaiah 26:3). When we trust God to see us through our challenging moments and draw close to Him, He takes away our anxiety and gives us true peace.

6. "Even to your old age, I am He, And even to gray hairs I will carry you! I have made, and I will bear; Even I will carry, and will deliver you" (Isaiah 46:4). We are God's beautiful creation; He made us and He loves us. No matter how old we get, God will carry us and take care of us.

7. "Blessed be the God and Father of our Lord Jesus Christ, who according to His abundant mercy has begotten us again to a living hope through the resurrection of Jesus Christ from the dead, to an inheritance incorruptible and undefiled and that does not fade away, reserved in heaven for you, who are kept by the power of God through faith for salvation ready to be revealed in the last time" (1 Peter 1:3–5). God gave us His most precious gift, His only Son, so that as believers we can live our days in hope, knowing that heaven waits for us. God's power protects us here on earth until we can finally claim our perfect, eternal inheritance.

CHAPTER 9

1. There are lots of reasons we can be reluctant to say no. Some of us are always excited to start something new. Some of us like to be needed. Some don't want to hurt someone's feelings or let someone down. Whether we just don't have a good reason to say no, or we feel obligated to say yes, it's easy to get overextended.

2. "See then that you walk circumspectly, not as fools but as wise" (Ephesians 5:15 NKJV). *Circumspect* is defined as "heedful of potential consequences" in the dictionary. A circumspect person is prudent and thoughtful, giving careful consideration to decisions before making them.

3. "For it is God who works in you both to will and to do for His good pleasure" (Philippians 2:13 NKJV). God loves us more than we can imagine, and His workings in and through our lives are for one main purpose—to bring glory to Himself, so that others may know Him and be saved. When you are faced with a decision, have you ever stopped to ask, "Will this bring glory to God?"

4. "What does the LORD your God require of you? He requires only that you fear the LORD your God, and live in a way that pleases him, and love and serve him with all your heart and soul" (Deuteronomy 10:12 NLT). This verse makes a good foundation for our decision-making process.

5. Our goals change with every season of life, but Christians of all ages should be committed to obeying God and doing His will. All of us have our own roles and responsibilities to manage, and God can be glorified when we fulfill them well. If we are spread too thinly, with too many responsibilities, we cannot do any one job well. We need to be focused on what's most important.

6. When you give yourself a chance to step back from the usual hustle and bustle, you'll have time to engage in activities that restore your peace and renew your spirit. Some options could be listening to soothing music, meditating, reading a good book, working on a jigsaw puzzle, praying, calling your grandparents, knitting, going for a walk, or spending time with family and friends. The possibilities are endless.

7. "What you ought to say is 'If the Lord wants us to, we will live and do this or that'" (James 4:15 NLT). Make God's will a priority in your decision-making process. Perhaps you can set up a rule for yourself, like waiting one full week before giving your answer to someone's request. Take that time to carefully assess your availability and pray for God's guidance.

8. "For you have need of endurance, so that after you have done the will of God, you may receive the promise" (Hebrews 10:36 NKJV). When we obey God's will and follow the path He has created for us, we will receive all the wonderful things He has promised us. So hang in there and do what you know is right. After all, eternity is just ahead.

SESSION 10

1. When we're anxious or stressed, we are easily ruffled by the unexpected. We're more likely to be critical of ourselves and others. But when we're ruled by the Spirit and not by our emotions, we put our faith in God rather than relying on our own strength, which allows us to face our circumstances with hope and optimism.

2. God didn't promise us an easy lot in this life. We will always be buffeted by some trial or another. So every one of us has *something* in our lives that pushes us the wrong way. Often, these things are simply out of our control. We can't change anybody else. Only God can do that. So when something beyond our control is the source of our turmoil, we can feel desperate because we can't *fix* the problem. However, we can make changes for ourselves. What do you need to let go of? Is it complaining, criticism, impossible expectations? When we begin to control our reaction to our stressors, our lives finally begin to feel a little calmer, even if the problem doesn't go away.

3. "With all lowliness and gentleness, with longsuffering, bearing with one another in love, endeavoring to keep the unity of the Spirit in the bond of peace" (Ephesians 4:2–3 NKJV). "Bearing with one another, and forgiving one another, if anyone has a complaint against another; even as Christ forgave you, so you also must do" (Colossians 3:13 NKJV). Even when we're frustrated and want nothing more than to complain, we are supposed to show one another the

love and forgiveness that Jesus has given to all of us. When we do as Christ would have done, we adopt His gentle Spirit.

4. It is very easy to pass judgment on other people for how they live their lives. We hang onto first impressions, we jump to conclusions, we make assumptions, and even worse, we pass them off as facts. Even well-intentioned folks can cause hurt feelings, emotional scars, and huge divisions in this way. Coming together as a Christian community is a wonderful thing, but we must be careful to guard ourselves against gossip. We are responsible to God for our own lives. We will answer to God for how we have lived. That is enough "business" to tend to without meddling in someone else's.

5. "Each of you has received a gift to use to serve others. Be good servants of God's various gifts of grace" (1 Peter 4:10 NCV). As Christians, our lives are woven together in the church. We are all a part of the same body. We are called upon to support one another, love one another, and encourage one another. That can all happen without meddling in each another's lives.

6. Hebrews 10:24 says "Let us think of ways to motivate one another to acts of love and good works" (NLT). The best way to motivate others to be loving and kind is by following the instructions in Ephesians 4:32: demonstrating Christ's love through your own words and actions.

7. There are those of us who could be completely happy to stay at home, in our own little world. Our relationship with God is one on one, and we're comfortable with that. Then there are those of us who thrive when we're surrounded by people. We have so much to share, and we live to pray with, encourage, and enjoy one another. God wants both of these qualities to be evident in our lives. We must strive for a balance.

SESSION 11

1. Sometimes our anxieties persevere. They seem to keep on coming back, no matter how much we'd rather they stayed where we put them. In the face of those anxieties and stresses, we must persevere in trusting God to take care of us.

2. "Be truly glad. There is wonderful joy ahead, even though it is necessary for you to endure many trials for a little while. These trials will show that your faith is genuine. It is being tested as fire tests and purifies gold—though your faith is far more precious than mere gold" (1 Peter 1:6–7 NLT). The unexpected happens in every life, and we often feel confused, flustered, shaken, even shattered. However, Peter assures us that these many trials are a way of proving that we trust God. The setbacks we deal with in this world are a means of testing our resolve. When we choose to trust God no matter what, He is glorified. And someday, we will receive His promise to us— inexpressible joy.

3. "Count it all joy when you fall into various trials, knowing that the testing of your faith produces patience. But let patience have its perfect work, that you may be perfect and complete, lacking nothing." (James 1:2–4). We will always experience trials and tribulations this side of heaven. But we are asked to be faithful, patient, even joyful in the midst of them. These trials give us a chance to choose again to follow God. They strengthen our patience and our character, which allows us to glorify God. That's one thing to be joyful about at least!

4. There are days when we *do* cry over spilled milk. Little annoyances add up until that last straw—the straw that broke the camel's back—shatters our resolve. Have you ever tried facing your smaller decisions and actions with the same earnestness and determination a large crisis would require? Don't let the little troubles grow into waves of anxiety or frustration. Pray for God's help to face them bravely, and with grace.

5. "Everyone who is a child of God conquers the world. And this is the victory that conquers the world—our faith. So the one who conquers the world is the person who believes that Jesus is the Son of God" (1 John 5:4–5 NCV). Do your best to let the little stuff go and keep the big picture in view. As Christians, we can rest in the promise that we will have victory in the end.

6. God's Word is a mirror for our hearts. It helps us to understand ourselves. It also helps us to know Jesus better. "If you abide in My Word, you are My disciples indeed" (John 8:31). Our lives are transformed only when we are abiding in the Scriptures. It may be easy to let your Bible reading slide from day to day, but in doing so you're only making it harder to create real, lasting change in your life.

7. The victory in our lives is not defined by our success, accomplishments, admirers, recognition, or self-confidence. Rather, a victorious life is one that brings glory to God. Be careful of your expectations, for God does not promise us an easy road. Life is hard, and there's no getting around that. But in the midst of our struggles, He has promised to be near to our hearts. He has promised to lift our burdens and carry us through. And "He who overcomes shall inherit all things" (Revelation 21:7). God will help us overcome our worldly troubles, and we will eventually inherit everlasting joy and peace. Things may not be perfect now, but we can rest in the knowledge that they are being perfected.

SESSION 12

1. "Whatever things are true, whatever things are noble, whatever things are just, whatever things are pure, whatever things are lovely, whatever things are of good report, if there is any virtue and if there is anything praiseworthy—meditate on these things. The things which you learned and received and heard and saw in me, these do, and the God of peace will be with you" (Philippians 4:8–9). Instead of focusing on the things that are going wrong, or the things outside of our control, we should make an effort to meditate on the blessings God has given us. When we give God praise for the things we're thankful for, our negative thoughts lose their power over us, allowing His wonderful peace to enter our hearts.

2. "In Me you may have peace. In the world you will have tribulation; but be of good cheer, I have overcome the world" (John 16:33). Jesus acknowledges that as long as we live in this earthly world we will have troubles. But we can face our problems with a sense of peace and optimism, knowing that our Savior will win in the end.

3. "Let the peace of God rule in your hearts. For as members of one body you are called to live in peace. And always be thankful" (Colossians 3:15). We have so much to be thankful for. God loves us and wants His own everlasting peace to rule in our hearts. Turn to Him the next time you're feeling anxious or stressed, and ask Him to help you live in His peace.

4. "Be anxious for nothing, but in everything by prayer and supplication, with thanksgiving, let your requests be made known to God; and the peace of God, which surpasses all understanding, will guard your hearts and minds through Christ Jesus" (Philippians 4:6–7). When we come to God in prayer, thanking Him for our blessings and asking Him to address our needs, we don't have to be anxious about what the future holds. We can rest in the promise that God will see us through it, and that He will grant both our hearts and our minds peace in the middle of life's confusion.

5. Romans 14:19 reads, "Let us pursue the things which make for peace." Though Jesus did purchase peace for us, we Christians should also pursue peace in our own actions. "Let him turn away from evil and do good; Let him seek peace and pursue it" (1 Peter 3:11). We have peace with God because of the shed blood of Jesus, but we need to actively pursue peace in our own lives with one another. And we do that by turning away from sin and striving to follow Jesus' example.

6. In 1 Thessalonians 5:13, Paul says, "Show them great respect and wholehearted love . . . live peacefully with each other." A good way to pursue peace in our own lives is to pursue peace with one another. We should show everyone the same love and respect that Jesus gives to us. Hebrews 12:14 also emphasizes the importance of extending peace to others: "Pursue peace with all people, and holiness, without which no one will see the Lord." Peace is more than just a worthy goal; it's a matter of eternal life or death!